BLEST BE THE TIE THAT FREES

KEN BERVEN

AUGSBURG PUBLISHING HOUSE

Minneapolis, Minnesota

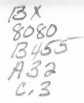
ACKNOWLEDGMENTS

While writing this manuscript, I called to mind those who have built their lives and experiences into my life, men I call with affection "The Chief," "Peter Bear," "Drews," "Braun," and a procession of others I leave unnamed. These are the men who caused me to understand the wonders and grace of God, the catalyst that the Holy Spirit used to make the message of this book alive in my experience. How thankful I am too for the labor of love (without complaint!) from my wife, Doris. Her encouragement and advice were indispensable.

BLEST BE THE TIE THAT FREES

CONTENTS

PREFACE

A crucial milestone in my journey came one day in 1969. I was landing at the San Francisco airport and had been reading my New Testament on the plane, searching for some answers for the immediate future. God spoke to me through His Word: "Let your way of life be free from the love of money, being content with what you have; for 'I will never desert you, nor will I ever forsake you.'" I read on with interest, "Remember those who led you, who spoke to you the Word of God; and considering the outcome of their way of life, imitate their faith. Jesus Christ is the same yesterday and today, yes, and forever" (Hebrews 13:5-8).

I believe God showed me from those verses that I was not to return to the business world on a daily basis, but to live on what I had and go to those who taught me the message of salvation.

It was in the Lutheran church that I met the Savior, not as an abstract Sunday figure, but as vital living person. It was here I was baptized, catechized, confirmed, and later married.

God did allow me to work among the congregations of the American Lutheran Church as a layman through the Commission on Evangelism. Although I was on a part-time basis for two years, I gave full-time service sharing my faith through a series called, "Renewal in Daily Living." God continued to supply all of our needs as he had promised.

Because of these experiences, I have felt compelled to write a book to do two things. First, to share the liberating truths I have learned and experienced in my walk with Christ and with other people just like me —people wanting to know God and appropriate His presence in their lives.

Secondly, to encourage the body of Christ to reassess its direction. Frankly, I am amazed how far many Christians have strayed into a works-centered theology. Even though we uphold grace as our dominant theme, we seem to have made a "work" out of grace.

I don't want to preach, I want to *share*. I don't wish to criticize, I wish to *suggest*. My motivation to write is to reach out through Christ to my brothers and sisters who first expressed their faith to me and say, "I really appreciate your help—and *you*." And then to say, "Hey, look. Is there a chance that there's more to this business of knowing Christ that we have missed? Maybe some things we have on paper, but have never put into practice can really be part of our daily lives with God."

1

Our Spiritual Portfolio

Ruth is a college friend who was spending the weekend at our house. It was Sunday afternoon, and several other people were joining us for dinner. The house was full of activity. A junior at an area college, she had recently left behind a life of depression and guilt and had turned on to a fascinating new life in Jesus Christ. There were still many symptoms of the old problems, but in Christ Ruth knew that she was free.

It was apparent that she was tense and nervous—she seemed to want to talk. The house with all its commotion was not the place for private discussion. I needed to have my car gassed and washed, and I invited her to join me.

As we drove to the station I asked her how she was getting along. She shared that she was constantly nervous and was disturbed about this new condition. As we were filling up with gas at the station, I asked her if she really knew what really was the source of her problem. After a few moments of reflection she said, "I guess it is because I keep looking at myself and my actions rather than Christ and who I am in Him."

I paid the attendant and drove over toward the car wash where we waited to ride through the giant machine.

"Why is it that I continue to have these problems?" she said. "I ask God to change me, but I just don't seem to see anything happen." The attendant began scrubbing the bugs off the grille as we waited at the entrance. Then the pulley-hook grabbed at the car, and the water began to spray. Then the soap. Before long the big brushes started rotating and came down gently on the hood.

About that time I said, "You know, this car wash operation is similar to the way that God works on us. I've already paid for the wash and wax job, but we are now in the process of receiving it. You pray and ask God to make you what you should be in Christ. He has already answered, but He is in the process of making it true in your experience."

By then we were to the waxing area, and the blowers soon blew all the water off the car.

As we came out into the sunshine, she said to me, "I see my problem. I know that I am in Christ, but I have allowed Satan to make me look at the failures of my flesh. I become nervous when I don't see my progress."

God says we have a spiritual portfolio that is "bullish" on our riches in Christ. He says that when we become Christians "all things have become new" (2 Cor. 5:17 KJV). My friend began to see that God is the one who must make that newness in our life true in our experience. She saw for the first time that living the Christian life is becoming what she has already been made. As she left for school that evening, she shared how earlier in the day she had experienced a great release through believing and allowing *God* to produce changes in her life.

Jesus Did It All

My experience with this student has been repeated many times over the years. Most believers live according to what they see in their lives. Since the day that I began to see myself as God sees me, I have been different. Before then, I always seemed to be trying to attain the standards that God had set for me. My experience, too, was to be introspective, and the result was failure and frustration.

The day that I believed what God said was true about me was the day I began to live in the freedom of being myself. I knew myself as being *in* Christ, and thus what was true about Jesus was also true about me.

What is true about me—and all of us who live in Christ? First, when God looks at us he sees us as saints. Holy ones. Paul writes to the Corinthians and says "to the church of God which is at Corinth, to those who

9

have been sanctified in Christ Jesus, saints by calling, with all who in every place call upon the name of our Lord Jesus Christ, their Lord and ours."

The people in the church of Corinth had outward evidences of sinful lives. Yet Paul writes to them and to Rome, Ephesus, Philippi—and to you and me— and calls us saints. The Holy Spirit inspired Paul to write this, and I cannot question His authority. In my experience I may not *feel* like a saint—a holy one— but as I believe God and allow the Holy Spirit to work in me, I find my life reflecting sainthood.

I also see that I can, like Paul, accept others this way. One of the great problems in the church and in Christian families is we have not seen each other as God sees us—as saints. If we cannot accept our fellow members of the Body of Christ as God does, then we are esteeming ourselves better than God—good luck!

Right-On Righteousness

The next truth I learned was that because I am in Christ, God looks at me and sees Christ. He sees me as He sees Christ. How does He see Him? As righteous in His sight. According to 2 Cor. 5:21 I have been made "the righteousness of God in Him." Romans 3:21-22 says that when we believed, we were made as righteous as God Himself. When God makes you righteous, He does a thorough job of it.

As I view myself from that perspective, I can cancel

out all of those inward feelings of unworthiness, unholiness and inconsistencies. God has laid heavy on me His righteousness, and by accepting this through faith I experience newness in Him. It is at this point that the Christian life starts to fall into place. I can see myself as "holy and blameless" because I am in Christ (Eph. 1:4).

When Satan attacks through his accusations and attempts to make me feel guilty, I can claim my position as holy and blameless in Christ. This act of faith releases God's power to make His life real for me.

I also see myself "blessed with every spiritual blessing in heavenly places in Christ (Eph. 1:3). Notice the verse says *in Christ*. How important when we feel a low spiritual ebb to see ourselves as *in Christ* blessed with all that we need spiritually. If we do not see ourselves this way, we try to make spiritual life happen by what we *do* rather than what we *are*. My student friend saw in herself no spiritual power or strength, and the more she tried to produce it, the worse the problem became.

It's like the situation we all experience time and again. The more we want something, and even demand it from the Lord, the less it seems to happen. I have found that the best way to live *in Christ* is to not work at it, but rather to claim the assets that are already mine and let Him produce the results in His time.

This principle of faith works in our human relationships, too. My wife has never really understood why people like me have to be overweight. (She's never had the problem; I can gain weight by reading a menu!) We had tension for years over my weight. One day she really transferred it over to the Lord and began to accept me as I was. The result was that with the pressure off, I became much more interested in my appearance and—though I seem always to be dieting—*I* am the one who wants to be different.

A Member of the Family

Knowing my position in Christ, I can see how God can "adopt me as His son." Because of Jesus Christ I can be chosen to be a member of His family. Jesus makes me acceptable to the Father.

During Biblical times adoption carried more serious implications than it does today. All "natural" members of a family could be disowned, but the adopted child could never be disowned. When I see myself as a permanent member of God's family, I am released from the position of trying to earn and maintain my position.

In a later chapter we will discuss the importance of the sacrifice of Jesus. But here let me say that seeing myself in Christ releases me from that "penance attitude" that had oppressed me for so long a time. My attitude was that whenever I did something wrong, I had better do something to cover that wrong or God would get even with me. The misery of living that way is immeasurable. I would castigate myself and do without something in order to cover my sin with my sacrifice. I was not willing (or did not believe) that Jesus' blood was sufficient to redeem me from *all* my sin (Heb. 10:14). Out of the riches of His Grace He had *lavished* his forgiveness upon us.

Lord, Help Me

Because I have been placed in Christ I have been endowed with "all wisdom and insight" (Eph. 1:8). This is not only for my spiritual life. Many times during a day I find this true in "secular" matters.

One time as I was working with some particularly difficult clients (we were planning their new offices), I had come to the end of my resources to present the kind of interiors they seemed to want. They were excitable people who were constantly talking to each other in Italian. I was frustrated. At a point in my presentation I excused myself and walked to the back of our showroom. I breathed a prayer, "Lord, you said if I lacked wisdom just ask for it. You said that 'because I am in Christ I am filled with wisdom and insight.' I'm going to depend on you to bring it out." By the time I entered our catalog room, I knew what would satisfy them. I returned and presented a completely new concept for their office. They left having placed an order for over seven thousand dollars.

In sharing this I do not suggest we should "trust Christ and grow rich." There are times when He chooses to exalt Himself through our lack of success. But often when I am talking to someone I find God gives me much insight.

God's Wisdom

As I was flying from Minneapolis to Chicago, and writing this chapter, the young man next to me seemed restless and in need. He evidenced the air of the young executive on his way up.

When we were landing he said, "You write large, and I couldn't help but notice what you were writing about."

He then proceeded to tell me of someone who had been sharing Christ with him, but could not answer his questions. We talked about these problems during our delayed taxi to the gate. As I left him in the airport lobby he said, "You're the first person I have never been able to outdo logically."

Many of his questions were answered. I wasn't trying to be logical. The Lord used this conversation to give me a fresh example of the endowment of wisdom and insight that is ours in the Spirit. I think that many of us are secret-service Christians because we don't think we will have the answers when we need them. God's promise is that He will give us the words to speak (Matt. 10:19-20). Why? Because in Christ we are filled with the wisdom of God.

The Will of God

Another blue-chip asset is that in Christ I am a possessor of His will (Eph. 1:9). It really bugged me for a long time because someone told me that in order to be in God's will I needed to be a "fulltime servant." That meant I needed to be a pastor, missionary, or church worker.

One day I learned that because I was in Christ I was in God's will already. I realized that God's will was not first what I *did* but first what I *was*. Paul said he prayed for the Colossians that they might be filled with the knowledge of His will (Col. 1:9). Later he said that God's will is that we be filled with the Holy Spirit (Eph. 5:17, 18). To me the mystery of God's will is to just abide in Christ (John 15) and allow His life to flow through me. When I am controlled by His Spirit, God's will is a natural result (Phil. 2:13).

I am doing today just exactly what I have always wanted to do—traveling and sharing my faith and freedom in Christ with others. My human reason said this might happen by the time I was sixty. God's will for me was that He updated my plans twenty years. Just by abiding and walking in Him, I saw His will and my will come together. I am learning not to push, just to trust.

I discovered that I did not have to run from meeting to meeting trying to get the Holy Spirit. Every place I went I heard a different plan, and I grew more confused. Finally I realized that when I believed, I was sealed with the Holy Spirit of promise given to me as a pledge of my ultimate inheritance (Eph. 1:13-14). I saw that I did not need to "get" the Holy Spirit. He had already "gotten" me.

Our Sixth Sense

The difference actually is that I now do not live only according to my own five senses. I believe that God gives us a sensitivity toward Him when we see ourselves as He sees us. My senses constantly draw attention to me. My new sensitivity is far more trustworthy than all my other senses combined. You see, the real me is not what my flesh tells me I am. I am living in a temporary world. This does not make me insensitive to what is going on around me. From that position I see myself as a quickened spirit. I am identified with and made one with God through Jesus Christ. What this does for me is to produce a whole new attitude toward life itself. I see that I have obtained an inheritance that is forever (Eph. 2:6). All of my possessions on earth are just props compared to what I have in store for me in the future.

Because I am identified with Jesus I have the riches of His grace (Eph. 1:11). It is not what I do for God, but rather what He does in me. It is no longer making promises to God, but allowing Him to fulfill His promises in my life. As with the car wash, I am in the process of receiving what has already been paid for—everlasting life—right now. My spiritual briefcase runneth over!

2

What's in a Name?

Names evidently were important to God—so important that when He created the first living being He named him "Adam," and delegated to him the task of naming every beast of the field and every bird of the sky. Whatever was brought before him, Adam named. Later, When God gave Adam a "helper suitable for him" he called her name "Eve."

In some books of the Bible we find catalogs of names: names of people; names of nations; names of tribes; names that are changed; duplicate names.

A Name Means Identification

When God told Moses to go to the exiled Hebrews in Egypt and tell of his experience at Sinai, Moses said he would have to know God's name. At that time this was a vital matter. It was popularly believed that there were many gods. The character or identity of a god or person was expressed in His name.

According to the narrative, God answered Moses: "I am who I am." Moses was instructed to tell the people, "I AM has sent me to you."

We learn the character of a person from his name. In Hebrew thought, the name is filled with mysterious power and significance, for the name represents the innermost self or identity of that person. Consequently, when a person went through an experience that changed or reoriented his life, he was given a new name.

Moses' question, then, represented an attempt to know the mystery of the divine nature, that is, the name of God.

Name of Names

God eventually gave one name that was so important that even today without it no one can have salvation. It is a name so powerful that it has been used to make the blind see, the lame walk, the deaf hear and the dumb talk. It is a name that is above every name—a name to which every knee will eventually bow.

Even the Jewish leaders recognized that there could be a significance in a mere name. Following the healing of the lame man in the temple, they asked the question of the disciples, "By what power, or in what name, have you done this?" (Acts 4:7) Throughout all time there has been no other name given that has the power of the name of Jesus.

I remember a Christian friend telling me of a situation in which he found himself tempted to commit adultery. He was traveling alone on Christian work to a country halfway around the world. He was a complete stranger to that area. Nobody knew him. He had already been away from home for over a month, and it would be several more weeks before he would be back home with his wife and kids.

Enroute on the plane, he struck up a conversation with another English speaking person, the stewardess. She was appealing and attractive, and he noted her interest in becoming better acquainted.

They landed at the airport, and he helped her through customs. She had mentioned she was scheduled for a 24-hour rest stop. They discovered they were to stay at the same hotel.

As they rode the taxi into town together, she offered to share her room with him. Everything was so simple. Who would ever know? And he was lonely beyond words. He had to decide one way or the other.

He helped her get her baggage from the taxi and into the hotel. But at that point he blurted out, "I can't do this. I—I work for Jesus Christ."

The whole desire was broken. He put her suitcases down in the hotel lobby, took his own bags back outside, caught a taxi and registered at another hotel.

The powerful name of Jesus had broken the temptation and set him free. He had appropriated God's authority over the matter through the name of Jesus Christ.

The Bible says that this powerful name has been given to men. He has placed that authority in our hands for us to use. Three times Jesus Himself repeats the words, "Ask in my name." What complete confidence He places in us to say "Whatever you ask in my name, that will I do" (John 14:14).

God Has No Grandsons

When I was born I was named Kenneth Alan to distinguish me from the rest of my family. We all had the name Berven. As I grew up I knew that I was part of the Berven family consisting of many relatives. Most of my family were believers. Even though I had been born into this family, I began to see that because I was a Berven and my parents were Christian, my salvation was not in our family name.

Not even the spiritual heritage of loving Christian ancestors could qualify me. I learned that I must personally claim the name of Jesus as my Savior. This seemed unnecessary at first because I grew up in an atmosphere of Christian love and acceptance. Prayer, Bible reading, thanksgiving were common wherever we went with our family or relatives.

In our church, personal faith in Christ for salvation was preached and believing was stressed. If anyone could have considered himself to be a Christian because of his social condition, it was I. But often I would hear the verse, "There is no other name under heaven that has been given among men, by which we must be saved" (Acts 4:12).

This began to get to me. Questions like, "Was I saved because I was a member of a family of Christians?", "Did being a Berven make the difference?", "Was I counting on my parents' and relatives' faith for my salvation?", began to plague me.

It was during this period of concern that this verse became meaningful to me. I kept hearing "There is no other name . . . but Jesus."

I saw for the first time that God has no grandsons.

This concern came to a climax while I was attending a convention in my early teens. Sometime during that week I believed in the name of Jesus as my personal Savior and trusted Him as my own. A settled feeling of assurance that I was a Christian followed that act of my will. It wasn't an emotional thing, just a matter of believing.

During the years that followed, the reality of believing in Jesus became more alive in my experience. I knew I was saved and that I belonged to God in a very special way.

Subtle Sidetracks

But like many people who come to faith in Christ from a Christian home, I found the simplicity of the gospel turn to something more complicated. I understood what it meant to be saved and to trust in Jesus, but Christian busy-ness slowly began to replace that simple walk of faith.

I became trapped in what was a subtle "theology of Christian activity and outreach" as a means of growth in Christ. I felt I was growing in my faith *because* I was so busy in many different church-related activities. I also fell into a superstitious religiosity that caused me to promise God almost anything, thinking I was being spiritual.

As an example, Martin Luther said at one point that he could not face the day without four hours of prayer. Because I wanted to be a man of God too, I felt I needed to pray before I faced my day—at least an hour. So I would get up early and pray and read the Bible the first thing in the morning. If some morning I would oversleep and miss my quiet time, I would live under self-imposed spiritual defeat in my life for that day. Of course I thought nothing of sleeping in late on Sunday morning. After all I was going to be in church most of the day anyway.

I began to make deals with God. I would beg God for forgiveness and promise Him I would not sin again. I would promise to love Him and serve Him if he would bless my business that day. I would promise Him that if He would get me through a bad day, I would even go out and do something special for Him, like witness to someone.

I was living with a code that said, "God expects me to do my part, you know." My Christian walk and acceptance before God was based on what I did each day, rather than on the work of the Holy Spirit.

In my own efforts I would try my best to discipline myself into a holy attitude, and inside I knew I was anything but holy. While around Christian people I was a model of the Christian. I carried my Bible to prove it. It became my badge that I was truly a spiritual man.

Rather than claim my forgiveness through the blood of Christ, I would deal with my sins based on my human ability to ward them off. I would try to neutralize the guilt by either humanly justifying sins or by condemning myself for having done them. This always resulted in an estranged walk with God. My superstitious religiosity provided no suitable program to deal with sin. Satan convinced me that by being my own police dog over sin I was being spiritual.

I also found myself in a trap that catches so many of us. My love and acceptance of other believers was based solely on the fact that we had a unity of purpose or commonness of doctrine, rather than on our oneness in Christ. For example, I felt there was only one Christian organization that had the answer to reach businessmen, so I joined it and promoted *it*. In Christian work, other organizations didn't seem to attract the caliber of people that *we* did. *My* church seemed to be the only one on the track. *Our* people were just a little better than those others down the street.

In each case I found it to be an attitude of pride which I excused because I thought everyone else in the group felt the same way I did. And all of us "unified" Christians couldn't have been wrong! If you weren't with us—well, God bless you brother, and see you around!

I had moved away from the centrality of the name of Jesus. Jesus Christ *is* the head of the church. Jesus Christ *is* the head of the Body. We are *all* sons and daughters of God and brothers and sisters in the same family, if we simply believe in Him.

It is to the name of Jesus that men will bow. It is the name of Jesus that produces a unity of purpose and belief.

Most believers have assumed that to be a Christian means that we must assume or maintain a certain lifestyle. We must pray. We must read the Bible. We must go to church. We must witness to our faith. We must lead a holy life. Because we bear the name of Jesus, we think we must be like Him, so we program ourselves by what other people do to be like Jesus.

When we look at the life of Jesus as recorded in the Gospels, nowhere does it tell us how He lived moment by moment. All we know about Jesus is that He did pray, He did witness, He was disturbed, He was compassionate, He was sorrowful, He was loving, He was obedient, He knew the Word of God, and He never did anything out of the will of His Father. He wasn't necessarily all of these things at any one time, though certainly He had the ability to be or do any one of them at any time.

This taught me a lesson. One time after realizing I had slipped into my works-based Christianity, I as an act of my will said to God, "I'm going to quit try-ing to produce the Christian life—you will have to do it for me." I transferred my trust to Him.

The relief was exhilarating. The weight and responsi-bility was off my back. I experienced freedom for the first time in a long time. I just relaxed in the Spirit.

Too Good to Be True—So I Re-Doubted

But as I began to see the results of that surrender, I became alarmed. I did not see myself praying very often. I didn't even read the Bible for a week. I did not tell anyone I was a Christian for a period of time. I thought about my relationship to Jesus often and was at peace with Him, but my whole mental attitude be-gan to be affected.

This surely could not be the Christian life I thought. It was too simple.

What I was doing was comparing what I was ex-periencing against what I thought the Christian life should be. I was not willing to accept just what God was doing in me. I wanted to live like Jesus, but even though I was trusting Him, I was not satisfied with the result.

So I began to *do* "Christian things" again. I made myself pray, read the Bible, and witness. And again I got bogged down. What I discovered was that al-though I had asked Jesus to live His life through me, what He was doing was not the mental picture of what I thought the Christian life should be. For so long I had been programmed by others to maintain a certain lifestyle that I could not handle the change. Now, that "mental picture" had to go. I had a lot to *un*learn.

He Has to Do It

Once again I was released in my spirit. I realized that whatever the Holy Spirit produced as a result of trusting Him I could accept as my lifestyle in Christ. He could produce obedience. He could give me a desire to pray, witness, fellowship or whatever. If none of it ever came as a result of my trust I could just go on believing in Jesus. God wanted me to name the name of Jesus as mine so I could live free from trying to be like Him in my own efforts.

My role as a child of the King is merely to trust Jesus to produce His life in me. In Him, I am a new person. The old is gone, and no longer is reality for me.

The result has been that I never read the Bible unless I want to. I never pray unless I want to. I never witness unless I want to. But, you know what? I just want to! Because it is no longer I who live, but Christ who lives in me.

Satan still comes and tries to get me to help God live the Christian life. He constantly reminds me that I must "do my part." But I've tried this route, and it's a bummer. I bear the name of Jesus Christ. I have His authority and power living in me. And on Him alone I choose to stand.

3

Where Love Begins

U.C.L.A. Psychologist, Dr. William Glasser, in his book *Reality Therapy* says there are two things necessary to live a successful life. The first is to be loved by someone, and the second is to live a life that is worthwhile.

As I interact with people from different backgrounds, I find that most in their own ways are searching for love. They want God and people to love and accept them as they are.

People try to find love in the world. They soon discover the world is really not a very lovely place. The question comes, "If God is love, how can I know it for sure? Is He *really* love?"

For sure, God is somewhat nebulous. You can't see Him, you can't touch Him, you can't feel Him, you can't put Him in a box. It's also impossible to *see* His love. God knew of our dilemma of not being able to detect Him through our five senses. That's part of the reason Jesus came. Jesus himself said, "I and my Father are One. If you have seen Me, you have seen the Father."

Really, the way we find out about God's love is through Jesus Christ and how He loved. Because He loves us, because we can know His love, our lives become worthwhile. Let's consider some examples of of His love.

Up a Tree

Take the story of the shady tax collector in Luke 19. Jesus had entered Jericho and was ministering to the people. Zacchaeus the tax collector had sold himself out to the Romans, the political enemy of the Jews, to collect taxes from his own people. He was probably the most hated man in town—the winner of "The Ugly Israelite" award as far as the rest of the people were concerned.

Jesus was there and he was walking along the road surrounded by all the "beautiful people" in town—the good Lutherans, Presbyterians, Baptists—everyone like us! The crowd was too tall and Zacchaeus was too short. He couldn't even see who Jesus was. So he ran on ahead to the fork in the road, and there climbed into a sycamore tree and waited to see Jesus as He walked by.

The Lord came walking along the road. He looked up into the tree and saw Zacchaeus. He said, "Zacchaeus, come down. I want to stay at your house to-day." Jesus singled out of that crowd the most unlovely person in Jericho. He picked him out as one he could show His love to, the man everybody else hated.

In fact, it is interesting who spoke first. Jesus made the first overtures toward Zacchaeus. He said, in effect, "Zacchaeus, in staying at your house today, I want to be your friend." He did not say, "What are you doing up there? Must you hide in that tree?" Jesus accepted him as he was. He could have said, "Zacchaeus, go off and get into the local church and then we will talk." He didn't say, "I'll tell you what. You go pay back all those debts to the people you cheated and then I'll come and stay at your house." No. He said, "Come down, I accept you just as you are."

And here we see God's love through Jesus Christ for you and me. He loves us exactly the way we are, and all he says to us is to come down into His fellowship. Come down into His lifestyle. Come and walk with Him.

Zacchaeus couldn't get out of the tree fast enough, could he? He came right down and they began to walk together along the road.

. . . "And when they (the crowd) saw it, they all began to grumble, saying, "He has gone to be the guest of a man who is a sinner." Who are the *they*? All the fine people. "Doesn't he know he is a sinner?" they murmured.

Zacchaeus said, "Stop the music! Hold it. Look, Lord, half of what I have I'll give to the poor. If I have cheated anyone or anything, I'll give them back four times as much."

Tell me something. Who told Zacchaeus to say that? He didn't need to have anybody tell him. He just wanted to. He wanted to do something because he had a new relationship with Jesus Christ. He had someone who loved him as he was. He had someone who accepted him. He wasn't worried whether he had money anymore. He wasn't worried about anything except to do what was right.

Zacchaeus was loved, and that's what changed him. He was accepted as he was. And what happened to him? He was changed. Jesus told the crowd, "Behold, salvation has come to this house, for he too is the son of Abraham." Why? Because he was willing to give everything back? No. Because he *believed*. He said, "Lord," and he believed in Jesus and he followed Him.

Caught in the Act

In John 8 is a story of a woman who was caught in the act of adultery, and the story of men who were her critical accusers.

The woman had, no doubt, been set up so they could nab her and bring her to Jesus, right in the midst of the temple where He was teaching—the very sanctuary where the law was kept to the letter.

They set her in front of Him and they said, "Here you are Jesus. We caught her. What are you going to do about it? The Law says stone her. What do you say?"

Jesus didn't lose his composure. He loved the accusers despite their criticism, and accepted the woman in all of her shame. He bent down and began writing on the ground. But they repeated their insistences again. "Come on Jesus, tell us what you're going to do. The Law says stone her. What do you say?"

Jesus stood up and said firmly, "Let him that is without sin cast the first stone."

The world was there trying to force Jesus to take sides. What a choice! Back-biting legalism *vs.* immorality. Love is when you give them both the choice of a third alternative: God's pardon and true forgiveness.

The Lord got to them. The accusers couldn't throw stones. One by one they started drifting off while He wrote on the ground again. Then he stood up and faced the woman. "Woman where are your accusers?" He asked.

And she said, "There aren't any, Lord."

"Neither do I condemn you," Jesus answered.

Now Jesus didn't say her sin was just. But he did say, "I don't condemn you. Go and from now on sin no more."

Why should He tell her that? Because He could give her the power to change. Had she not been willing to trust Him, His telling her to sin no more would only have made her a worse adulterer. But she said "Lord," and she believed on Him. She possessed a brand-new life.

A lot of us get disturbed when someone like this meets Christ and comes into our fellowship. We mentally turn them off. Yet, Jesus came for these people. This story tells us they are no worse than we are! He loves the puritan and the prostitute the same.

Ol' Mighty Mouth

Have you ever denied Jesus? Join the club. We all sometime in our Christian life have denied Jesus. In John 13 we read about Peter, the man who spoke before putting his brain in gear. He seemed to challenge most everything Jesus said. In fact, I think he had to open his mouth to change feet. He was always popping off about something.

And here he was standing before Jesus saying, "I'll never deny you, Lord."

Have you ever made a promise to God? Did you fully keep it? You know what promises to God do? They commit your flesh to try harder. God doesn't want our promises. He wants our trust!

Peter the fisherman had been born and raised in an atmosphere where the Law of Moses was the rule of his home. He and Andrew his brother were taught that the hope of Israel would be the Messiah, the deliverer. When Andrew met Jesus and believed Him to be the Son of God, his natural response was to bring Peter to meet the Savior. As these brothers became disciples, Jesus singled out Peter as a spokesman and even entrusted to him a key role of building the church on earth.

Peter had extreme difficulty shaking all his early

legalistic training. As Jesus would speak of a life of faith without works or performance, Peter's nature was to rebel verbally.

For example, one day Jesus was with his disciples (John 13:1-11). They had just finished eating. Jesus rose, and as he wrapped a towel around himself, assumed the role of a servant. He poured water into a basin and began to wash the disciples' feet. He washed Bartholomew's, John's, James', Judas' and on until He came to Peter.

Peter had been watching this whole scene, and the thought kept running through his mind, "How can the Son of God wash my feet?" The early training kept filtering through. "*I'm* supposed to be serving and doing something for *God*. He should not be serving me."

Jesus approached Peter with the basin. Ol' Mighty Mouth could not contain his emotions. He blurted out, "Lord, do you wash my feet? Never shall you wash my feet!"

Then Jesus gently and in love answered Peter, "If I do not wash you, you have no part with me."

That totaled Peter out. He wanted to be part of Jesus. After all, He was the promised Messiah. He wanted to be a complete believer. But here was Jesus in love offering to serve him. Peter was overwhelmed.

Peter was beginning his exposure to living by faith. It wasn't his promises to Jesus, but Jesus' promises to him that really counted. He had only one response. "I'll ask Him to wash my hands (so my service might be clean) and my head (so my thoughts will be pure) instead of just my feet."

Peter learned the principle that *faith means never having to say, "I promise."* Knowing Jesus is not a matter of man promising, but of man trusting in God's promise. And this explains why Peter wrote toward the end of his life that we are "protected by the power of God through faith" (1 Peter 1:5). How beautifully simple it is for us to walk with Christ!

4

Getting a Head in the World

In the late sixties the lyrics of a popular song said, "What the world needs now is love, sweet love; not just for some, but for everyone."

The songwriter expressed the longing and desire of many a heart since the beginning of time. "Why can't people just get together and love each other?" is a common question. Bumper stickers say, "Make Love Not War." People are becoming "love conscious" in their relationships with others.

Jesus made it clear that there was virtue in our love of God, love of self, and love of others. He said, "A new commandment I give to you, that you love one another, even as I have loved you, that you also love one another" (John 13:34). Jesus' life and ministry evidenced the fulfillment of His own commandment.

We have seen how Jesus' love changed the course

of the life of Zacchaeus, the adulterous woman, and Peter. In the first century many people met their deaths because of that life-changing love. Many became transformed by experiencing the love of God through other members of the Body of Christ. People began to come alive to the love of Christ which surpassed knowledge (Eph. 3:19). Jesus said others would know His disciples because of their love for one another (John 13:35).

Christ Said We're His Body

I began to experience the love of Christ which surpasses knowledge in a unique way. Some brothers and I were spending considerable time together in prayer and Bible study. We were learning together about the Body of Christ and its function.

As we studied it became apparent that the "glue" that held the Lord's people together was Christian love and mutual acceptance. The disciples and the early church seemed to be not only one in the spirit, but also one in their relationship to each other.

We began to see the reason was the Body's relationship to the Head. In all things the Body honored the Head, Jesus Christ. No one placed himself in a superior position to the other. Jesus was the Head, and all the members were willing subordinate members.

We also found that members each had a function (gift) for the Body's good. No one, therefore, was any better than the other. No one had more leverage than the other. With this kind of a relationship, it became apparent that love and acceptance came as a result of knowing who they were as members of Christ's Body.

This taught me a very valuable lesson. I saw that I could accept myself as I was and did not have to be concerned about other people and their better abilities. I was learning something about loving myself.

Many times I had been taught that "in me dwelleth no good thing," so my tendency was to put myself down. But that passage (Rom. 7:18) is talking about the fleshly, not the spiritual man. Sure there is nothing in old nature that is good. But I found that as I believed God for the new man He made me, I began to change.

I changed in my relationship to other believers. Where before my desire was to attempt to be better, and to brag about all that I had accomplished, I began to accept the achievements of my brothers and sisters with pride and satisfaction. When someone was praised for a spiritual victory, I considered it mine as well. I was part of them and they were part of me. And what a difference love has made in my attitude toward myself. I don't have to be something that I am not. I can love and accept myself because I know who is the Head of the Body.

As I allowed Jesus to be the head of my life each day, I experienced tremendous release. With an attitude of dependence upon Him, I find Him guiding and directing me. Just as my physical head controls my body, Jesus also controls my life daily.

But Jesus is more than a Head over individuals. He

is Head of the Corporate Body—and not just theologically, either. He literally wants to control His Body on earth. As I see the Christian life, it is a life of people believing and loving, a life where faith is directed toward God alone for everything. The result, then, is a life of love directed toward others. It is a life of faith in God resulting in a life of love and ministry to others.

Love Really Works

A number of years ago a couple who were close friends left our church to join with a group to form a new local church. They were excited about their fellowship and often encouraged us to join with them. They were confident they had found *the* church and wanted everyone to experience what they had. We visited their meetings several times and felt they had a great fellowship, but we didn't share the same exuberance over their group as being any better than all the other things God was doing with His people.

Our friends began to get more and more involved in their new church group. We saw less and less of them. This was a surprise to us because we had had such a close relationship previously. Finally we did not have any contact with them unless we initiated it. Those contacts were cordial, but never as they had been before.

A year or more passed, and the relationship from their side made an abrupt turn. We seemed to be back to the close spiritual and friendly times we had had before. My wife and I had made no effort to pull things back together. We just enjoyed these friends and were thrilled things were back to normal again. They had not left their church; they were more deeply involved than ever.

Six months later the husband was visiting in our home one morning. We began to talk about his church group. He expressed to us how the teaching of this church had caused them to think of themselves as better than we—that because they were *"the* local church" all other believers were to be avoided and true fellowship could only be found in that group.

Then our friend volunteered why he had resumed the relationship with us again. He said, "My wife and I began to notice that on every contact we had with you, you folks just kept on loving us. As a result we began to notice more love in being with you than with some of our church group."

Doris and I were amazed. We were consciously making no effort to show any special love to them during those days of separation. Any love we showed to them came as a natural result of trusting Jesus Christ. God was just fulfilling what Paul said to the Romans that "the love of God has been poured out within our hearts through the Holy Spirit who was given to us" (Rom. 5:5).

Love is part of His life within us—not something we work at. We did not feel ourselves better or in-ʿerior to our friends. They were members of the Body of Christ just like all other believers, and the Head had them fellowshiping somewhere else.

As a member of Christ I can experience Jesus' love everyday. I can express it then to others. His love just comes naturally through the Holy Spirit.

The Way That He Loves

How does He love me? He loves me with a love that understands me. He knows where I am at. Jesus knows what life is all about. He lived here on earth. He is not a Savior that cannot identify with our weaknesses. When other people cannot understand us, Jesus does and He loves us with infinite understanding. I too can appropriate this love for others as I trust the Head of the Body.

I also find that He loves me with a love that really cares for me. Peter encourages us to cast "all your anxiety on Him, because He cares for you" (1 Peter 5:7). This ego-centered world is not a place where people are concerned for one another. But He cares, and as I trust Him, He cares through me as well. My concern and empathy for others comes from the Head.

He loves me with a love that wants to provide. So many times I see God not only provide for my needs, but even for my wants. Out of His love for me He wants to give me what I desire. As I trust Him, I see Him cause me to want to provide for others. My motivation to do this comes from love, not compulsion.

As we study the life of Jesus, we find that His life

was a life of faith, too. He trusted His Father and the result was a life of love for others. He went around seeing how He could fulfill the needs of other people. If He met people who were sick, He would heal them. If He saw a person in need, His love motivation caused Him to want to fulfill that need. Whether it was to fulfill some temporal or eternal need, Christ was motivated by a love which produces an active response.

The same choice is ours today as believers. As a member of the Body of Christ, we have a Head. That Head is Jesus. He is our source of wisdom, power, intellect, and direction. To get a Head in the world is to get Jesus into everything we do.

Think of what you have because you are a Christian. You have a "together" Head who can do all things. Yet with all this tremendous power, He ministers to our needs. What a privilege to be a part of the Body of Christ!

5

Why Love Is Possible

Years ago a wise old Christian gave me a piece of advice. He said, "Beware of those who outwardly appear pious, because they would likely lie to you about other things as well." Recently I saw this statement have real meaning.

My wife and I decided to attend a morning church service where a friend of ours was speaking. At the end of the service I was called to the platform to dismiss the meeting in prayer.

Following the service as we were visiting with friends, a man approached us. Though I had not seen him in over ten years, I remembered him as one of the leaders in the religious community. He was a respected university professor, an elder in his church, and a Bible teacher. He was the kind of man most Christian leaders sought out for help to interest others in their work.

As he introduced himself to me, it was evident that he did not remember me or Doris. He said, "You mentioned something in your closing prayer that hit on a problem area in my life." We shook hands and I introduced Doris and myself.

I wasn't even sure he caught our names, but he immediately went on to say, "You said, 'God, it's not the promises that we make to You, but the ones that You make to us that count.' I've never thought of it that way before." He then commented, "I've made so many promises to God that I cannot even remember them to know if I've kept them."

Later that week I received a phone call from the man, inviting me to lunch. As we dined together he poured out a story of defeat as a Christian which was anything but what he evidenced outwardly. He told me things about himself that I'm not sure he had ever shared with anyone. In his desperate search for peace in his life, he had sought me out as one who could possibly help him.

He expressed some real doubts about his relationship to God, and that he was never sure he was good enough to be on "praying ground." His problem seemed to center around whether he had surrendered himself totally to God in everything. His faith, therefore, depended upon whether *he* had enough spiritual power for each situation.

This "pious man," like so many of us, was outwardly a shining example of a "together" Christian, but inwardly he knew that he was not. He confessed to me his life of lies and deceit to the Christian community and to himself.

It's That Same Old "Sindrome"

One dominant note in our conversation was his consciousness of sins in his life—sins of the past that troubled him, his sin of deceit to others with his bogus life style. He shared how he would have victory over sin for a while. Then he would sin, and devastating guilt would return. This guilt feeling in his life often brought him to the point where he would doubt his salvation.

As I listened to this man's lament, I recognized how many of us put up false fronts, too. In our desire to please God we are led into a trap of making bargains with God to keep us from sinning. Then when we do sin, we begin to doubt *our* "Christian strength." We begin to examine ourselves and the result usually causes us to put on masks which cover up our imperfectness.

Probably the greatest cause of this problem is that we have forgotten that Christ has already placed God's children in right standing with our Father. We attempt to deal with our sins by what *we* do through penance or self-condemnation. This troubled man, like so many of us, was not aware of Christ's total work of redemption through His blood.

I told this man what I knew and had experienced about living in the freedom of my Christian life. He

listened eagerly. He wanted help. Yet he was so programmed to earn his salvation that he left that lunch
still bound up in his human performance.

This man, like so many, was longing to be free from
guilt and shame but was afraid to believe that he was
forgiven of all sins—past, present and future.

Jesus' Payment Was Complete

Why can I make such a bold statement? How can
I be so sure that we can live in a forgiven state continually?

God knew that man would experience this problem
of a consciousness of sin. He knew that the Accuser's
tactics would cause men to be sin-centered in their
lives. As a result, God in his grace, dealt a final blow
to the Accuser on our behalf once and for all. Ephesians 1:7 says, "In Him [Jesus] we have redemption
through His blood, the forgiveness of our trespasses,
according to the riches of His grace, which He lavished
upon us."

Why is the blood of Jesus so important to us today
nearly two thousand years later? Because God requires
a blood sacrifice for sin (Heb. 9:22). We as believers
have been redeemed by the blood of Jesus and *are
being* forgiven by that blood daily.

Preview of Coming Attractions

The importance of the blood of Jesus became clear
to me as I understood the Old Testament sacrifice

system. When I saw it as a "shadow of the good things to come," I too began to experience what it means to no longer have a "consciousness of sins" (Heb. 10:2). As a result I learned to experience by faith Christ's cleansing on a continuing basis.

When Moses was on Mount Sinai God told him to build a tabernacle in the desert. This was to become a place of worship for the Israelites. The Israelites were to bring to the priests an animal to be slain, and its blood was to be sprinkled on the altar just inside the entrance to the tabernacle. There were many priests who performed this order of sacrifice daily on behalf of the people who came.

Suppose you were an Israelite who came to have your sins forgiven. You would find in your herd a perfect animal that you would bring to the priest for sacrifice. You would confess your sin to the priest. You would then kill the animal by slitting its throat. The priest would take the blood of the animal into the tabernacle and sprinkle the blood on the first altar. Having met God's requirement, he would return and declare you forgiven of your sin. Then you would leave knowing that God's requirement for your sin had been met.

But if you sinned again the next day you would have to return and go through the whole process all over again. This was the basis by which you could be forgiven and have true absolution of your sin. Now if you were a big sinner and were penitent every time, it could get tough on the livestock supply!

In addition to these regular sacrifices for sin, God ordained that once a year a sacrifice would be made by the High Priest on behalf of all of the people. This sacrifice was for all of their sins for all of the year. This annual meeting was called Yom Kippur, the day of atonement. It was a time when the whole nation could be at one with God. No sin was held against anyone at the time of the annual meeting. The High Priest had to perform the sacrifice because he had his own sins to deal with as well.

While the High Priest was in the Holy of Holies before God, the whole nation was in a forgiven state before God. None of the people were alienated from God because of their sins. All were forgiven and covered. It was during this period of time they could experience no consciousness of sin: they were being covered by the blood sacrifice. What a relief to know that all their sins done in ignorance, the sins done willfully, the sins that hurt others—all sins were cancelled out by the sacrifice. The blood had done the job. The High Priest had met God's requirement. It was an exciting day.

Jesus Christ: Our High Priest

There were problems that presented themselves. First, the High Priest could not remain in the Holy of Holies permanently. He had to come out. Secondly, the blood of the animal covered the sins previously committed, not for the future. This meant they always needed a new animal each year. Thirdly, when the High Priest came out of the Holy of Holies, the children of Israel were on a new year and had to return to the basis of daily sacrifice for sins. A fourth problem was that the High Priest himself needed to be replaced at intervals because of death.

The great liberating truth taught in the New Testament is that Jesus Christ became "the good things to come." In each of the above four problem areas Jesus Christ was the answer to the dilemma. He became our perfect Sacrifice. He dealt with the sins of all men for all time, not just for one year. We do not need another blood sacrifice. John the Baptist declared when he saw Jesus, "Behold the Lamb of God that takes away the sins of the world." He received and uttered this divine revelation nearly four years before it actually happened.

As "the real thing" Jesus has become our perfect high priest. He never has to be replaced because of death. He did not have to perform the sacrifice because of His own sin. He did it willingly on our behalf because of His love for us.

Jesus Christ is also in the Perfect Holy of Holies which was pictured in the Old Testament tabernacle. Jesus Christ is today before the Father—at his right hand—interceding for our sins as our perfect high priest. He is there with the perfect sacrifice, His own blood, because of the eternal redemption He has made on our behalf.

The light went on inside me when I realized Jesus

was still in the Holy of Holies. He has never come out since He returned to God's throne from earth. He, therefore, is always before the Father. Comparing the Old Testament lesson and this truth, I saw that while the temporal high priest was in the Holy of Holies the people were not guilty or conscious of sins. They were conscious, rather, of the sacrifice. Then all the more true is the fact that I, too, need not experience guilt, alienation, or a consciousness of sin. Jesus Christ is there in the "eternal tabernacle not made with hands" with his own blood to appear in the presence of God for me (Heb. 9:11-12).

The children of Israel experienced total forgiveness *once a year*. We can experience total forgiveness *forever!* Because sin was dealt with forever. We are not alienated from God because of sin. First John 1:7 says that "the blood of Jesus His Son cleanses us from all sin." And if I do sin, Jesus' blood is actually cleansing me before the Father even while I am in the act of sinning.

The annual meeting has now become a one-time meeting with everlasting results. Jesus is always before the Father. We do not need anyone else. This truth sets me free from a consciousness of sin. God has put sin out of His mind, and so can I! (Heb. 10:17). I can serve the living God and be myself. I do not have to be an imposter Christian. I can allow others to see me as I am—a man made whole who lives in His forgiveness with a conscience being cleansed daily through the blood of Christ.

I now see Jesus sitting at the right hand of the Father, not as my Judge, but as One who is interceding for me and reigning over me and living in me and through me. I do not have to notice my sin. I feel no terror or regret in my conscience because of sin. My life is hid with Jesus Christ, the Son of God, the High Priest, the perfect sacrifice, and I am identified with Him forever.

6

It's Just Not the Issue

At a youth congress I had an opportunity to meet a friend who had been a great communicator of the gospel to young people. As part of the Jesus Movement he related to the needs of the young through his singing and speaking the message of Christ. Many met the Savior through his clear-cut presentations.

When we met at the Congress, he had not sung publicly in six months nor was he fellowshiping with other believers. We talked briefly about his problem and why he was not carrying on his ministry. He indicated he could not see how he could be used of God on one hand and find his life so full of sin on the other. Because he could see himself walking in darkness, he finally decided just to quit trying to change himself until he could figure out a way to overcome his problem.

At the end of the meetings I discovered that we were to fly to San Francisco on the same plane. As we took off, he said to me, "What can I do about my problem? I'm more complete when I'm living out my faith, but I seem to be constantly defeated by sin."

For the next hour as we shared together from the Scriptures, he saw that the reason he was walking in darkness and not free was because he had forgotten he was forgiven. I shared the story of Christ as our great high priest, constantly keeping us clean from sin, and the light of life dawned on him. He saw himself as totally forgiven. When we landed in San Francisco my friend confessed that he really knew he was cleansed of all his sins. He said he felt he had returned to that time when he had first received Christ and experienced absolute forgiveness.

I invited him to spend the rest of the summer with us in Seattle and learn more about God's grace and forgiveness. He accepted my invitation and became an eager student and proponent of Christ's total work on the cross. Though he was never beyond temptation to sin, he never again experienced the guilt and darkness he had known previously. Why? He believed that the blood of Christ truly cleansed him. Jesus said, *and meant it,* that He was the light of the world. When we know Him and His completed work for sin, we then *experience* the light of life.

Freedom and Forgiveness

Paul, as he wrote to the Galatians, said, "It was for freedom that Christ set us free: therefore keep standing firm and do not be subject again to a yoke of slavery." The yoke of slavery Paul refers to here is the bondage of slavery to the impossible demands of the Law. Yet it was Jesus who said, "I am the light of the world; he who follows Me shall not walk in the darkness, but shall have the light of life" (John 8:12). People all over this world are looking for a life of light and reality. They're looking for a life that has meaning and purpose, a life that is full, a life of peace and stability instead of guilt.

God wants to communicate to this world His message of love. He wants to communicate His message of acceptance, His message of forgiveness, His message of power, His message of peace which can transform those who are troubled. I really believe that when people misunderstand the totality of Christ's forgiveness they experience defeat due to sin in their daily living.

Paul said we could be free. Jesus said we could know and experience a life of light. The question is, how do we get there? How do we make this true in our daily experience?

The Holy Spirit makes it very clear that if you are a Christian, if you as an act of your will have invited Jesus to be your Savior, that all of your sins—past, present, and future—have been forgiven. "Of Him all the prophets bear witness that through His name every

53

one who believes in Him has received forgiveness of sins" (Acts 10:43). The basic thrust of the gospel is that sin is no longer the issue with God, and that we as forgiven people can live in that cleanness day by day.

This is not to say that the cross brings no human response, that everything is automatic. It is to say, however, that Jesus paid for the sins of the world. For example, I could invite you to lunch and pick up the tab. The meal is paid for. Whether or not you choose to eat your lunch is up to you. It's yours for the taking. The barrier of price has been removed. It's completely paid for. There is nothing you can do to earn the meal. It's free! The issue is no longer the lunch. The issue is whether or not you're going to enter into the act of eating it.

In a similar way, sin—yours and mine—was paid for by our Lord Jesus Christ on the cross. All of it. He missed nothing.

Everyone who believes in Jesus has received forgiveness of sins—*all* of them! My question to you is, do you believe that? And look what Paul says in quoting David: "Blessed are those whose lawless deeds have been forgiven, and whose sins have been covered. Blessed is the man whose sin the Lord will not take into account" (Rom. 4:8). As God looks down upon you and me and sees us through the cross, He sees us dressed up in the righteousness of Jesus. He sees us *forgiven*. Our problem is that in our experience, in our lives, we see our sins—right? And Satan will back you up on that to the hilt! It's what he wants you to think.

You see, Satan is the accuser of the brethren and he goes to God and he says, "Look at what Ken did!" But Jesus says, "By blood covers that, Father," and Satan gets nowhere with God. The devil comes to us with his old reminder. "You did it again, didn't you? You promised God you wouldn't do it." He comes in and accuses over and over. But if you *know* you're forgiven of all your sins, that they are all covered by Christ's blood, that you are literally *in* Christ—you can say, "Satan, you liar, I know I'm forgiven."

Sin just isn't the issue. Because of Christ, you can abound in the absolute forgiveness that is yours. And that's not taking your forgiveness for granted, either. It's just living in what God says is true about you.

Faith and Forgiveness

I am convinced that the place from which God begins to cause us to grow in our lives as Christians (and this is what has changed my own Christian life) is when we begin to *believe our forgiveness*. In 1 John 2 we find why it is that God can say our sin is cancelled. "And He Himself is the propitiation (payment) for our sins; and not for ours only but also for those of the whole world."

Now certainly if the whole world's sins are paid for, mine must be part of them. Every man's sin has been cancelled. There isn't one person who ever lived or who ever will live whose sin was not paid for at the cross. Jesus paid for the sins of the people who lived before the cross, and He paid for those who lived after the cross.

In Hebrews we read that when Jesus died He died once and for all for all time and satisfied God for all man's sins. In 2 Corinthians 5 we come across the word "reconciled." Reconciled means "to bring back together." "Namely, that God was in Christ reconciling the world to Himself, not counting their trespasses against them, and He was committed to us the word of reconciliation." Paul says that God was in Christ on the earth bringing men and Himself back together again.

Now look at what else the Apostle says: "not counting their sins, their trespasses, against them." God is literally not even holding sin against the world. What is He then confronting the world with? Believing in Jesus. *Jesus, not sin, is now the issue.* "For God did not send the Son into the world, not to condemn the world, but that the world might be saved through Him. He who believes in Him is not condemned; he who does not believe is condemned already, because he has not believed in the name of the only Son of God" (John 3:17-18 RSV).

Our problem as Christians is that often we tell people only that they are sinners. True. But what else do we need to tell them? That they are forgiven, that God has done something, that He has dealt with the source of their problem. When the statement is made that no man is going to hell for sinning, it's really true. Man is separated from God in this life and in the life to come *because he does not believe in Jesus.*

Years ago the newspapers carried a story of a young man sitting in a prison in New York State. He was condemned to die for murdering three women. One day the officials came to tell him that his parents had fought his case in the courts, and his sentence of death was commuted to life imprisonment. But he refused the pardon. This had never happened before. He said, "I should pay for my crime with my life."

They didn't know what to do. They took the case to the United States Supreme Court, and the Court ruled that a pardon is not a pardon until it is received.

Tell me, has every man's sin been paid for? Has every man's sin been pardoned? Has Jesus paid the debt? Certainly! But when does it become reality? When we believe it—when we take Christ at His word.

You see, not every man is going to go to heaven. Jesus talked about heaven being sparsely populated. I'm talking about those who believe in Jesus Christ. They have accepted or received their pardons. Our trusting Jesus is what God is after because Jesus took sin out of the way.

The Result Is Righteousness

And here is another ramification. I find that when I became less sin-centered and more Christ-centered, I began to sin less. Remember the truth of Isaiah 53:6:

"All we like sheep have gone astray; we have turned every one to his own way; and the Lord hath laid on him the iniquity of us all."

Imagine that I am holding a handful of coins and these coins represent all of my sins. Let's say my left hand represents me. For the sake of our illustration, the right hand represents Jesus Christ. Let's read the verse again. "All we like sheep have gone astray; we have turned every one to his own way; and the Lord hath laid on him the iniquity of us all." I take the money from my left hand and pour it into my right hand. The left hand is empty and free. Our sins have been laid on the Lord Jesus. How many are gone? How about your worst sins? Are they on Jesus? The habitual ones? Have they been laid on Jesus? Isn't that tremendous!

You know what? God has already forgotten the sins you are going to commit tomorrow. So why should you get hung up about them? Why even do them? Who do you think wants you to be sin-centered? The enemy of your life, Satan. God has made you free from sin through the blood of Christ.

Signed, Sealed, and Paid For

At the time the Bible was written, if a man was put in prison a piece of parchment was nailed to the door of his cell and on that parchment were listed the decrees against him—robbery, murder, rape, or whatever it might have been. If he lived long enough to be set free from the jail sentence, he was given this parchment as a certificate of debt proving his payment for his crime to the Roman government. Across that certificate of debt, once he had fully served his sentence, was written the Greek word *tetellestai* meaning, literally, "paid in full."

That is why Paul wrote in Colossians 2:13-14: "And when you were dead in your transgressions and the uncircumcision of your flesh, He made you alive together with Him, having forgiven us all our transgressions, having cancelled out the certificate of debt consisting of decrees against us and which was hostile to us; and He has taken it out of the way, having nailed it to the cross. When Jesus Christ died on the cross among His last words He said were, "It is finished." The literal word he cried out was "tetellestai"—it is finished, paid in full, once and for all. And your sins are covered!

Now consider Romans 8:1: "There is therefore now some condemnation for those who are in Christ Jesus." Is that right? "There is therefore now, no condemnation for those who are in Christ Jesus. For the law of the Spirit of life in Christ Jesus has set you free from the law of sin and of death." There is no condemnation now or ever if you are in Christ. God says that you are in Jesus Christ. You are dressed up in Jesus Christ, and there is nothing going to come into your life that first does not pass through Jesus Christ. And God literally looks at you and sees Jesus Christ.

Let me personalize 2 Cor. 5:21. "God made Christ who knew no sin to be sin on Ken's behalf that Ken might become the righteousness of God in Christ." How righteous is God? He is absolute righteousness, righteousness raised to the highest power. And God says I'm the same way. Heb. 10:14 says, "For by one offering He has perfected for all time those who are sanctified." He has made you perfect forever. Can you improve on what God calls perfect? Good luck! All the time that we work at trying to be better, God already sees you perfect in Christ.

If you believe you are a bad student, you probably make poor grades. If a man doesn't think he is able to farm his land effectively, he will have a problem with his crops. If a boy believes he will be a poor athlete, he probably will not go out for the team. And if a woman doesn't think she's a good cook, I don't want to eat her food!

Because we live according to what we think we are, we become what we think. If you think you are a dirty, rotten sinner, you probably are. That's what you are thinking about. Many of us live from the wrong perspective. We as believing Christians have so often just absolutely forgotten that God has changed us. He sees you as perfect. He sees you as a member of his family. He sees you as being in Christ.

Tailor-made Forgiveness

One day on a trip around the world, I came into Hong Kong by plane. A young Chinese man was there meeting people to interest them in his business in

Kowloon. He came up to me and said, "I have a tailor shop downtown. We can make you a suit in one day. May I invite you to my shop?"

I told him I would like to see what he could do, but would not be able to come until nine o'clock that evening. He agreed to pick me up in his car at nine, and I was to bring along as many of my traveling companions as I could interest.

Before he left I gave him a copy of a little booklet I had been using to share my faith as I traveled in other countries. I suggested he read the booklet and let me know what he thought of it when he picked me up at nine. In the booklet it explains about God's love, His forgiveness, and how to receive Christ. We made our date, and he promised to read the booklet.

About a quarter to nine the phone rang at my table in the dining room. It was Jimmie Sung and he was in the lobby already. I told him I was still eating, and I would be down by nine. He apologized but said he had come early to talk about the booklet.

He said, "Mr. Ken, I read the booklet, and it said something that I want to know about."

I excused myself and went down to the lobby of the hotel and met him. His first statement was, "Mr. Ken, I want you to know that I am not religious. I have no religious background at all. But that booklet said something that I want to know about."

I went through the plan of salvation again with him and asked him if he would like to have Jesus come into his life. He agreed and together by the telephone booths we prayed, and Jimmie Sung invited Jesus to be his Savior. As I gave him assurance, I shared how Christ had really come into him, that he was assured of heaven, and that all of his sins were forgiven.

About nine o'clock some of the other travelers came to join us, and we got into Jimmie's car and drove over to his shop. I was sitting alongside him. As he was driving along he looked over at me and said, "Mr. Ken, do you mean to tell me that all of my sins, even the ones that I can't tell my wife about, are forgiven?" And I said to him, "That's right Jimmie." Jimmie let out a sigh of relief that was audible to every one in the automobile.

Jimmie had experienced in his forgiveness the cleansing of salvation that John describes: "If we confess our sins, He is faithful and righteous to forgive us our sins and to cleanse us from all unrighteousness" (1 John 1:9). Jimmie had been cleansed from all his unrighteousness, and knowing it caused him to experience tremendous relief.

I come across many Christians, who have experienced anew the joy of living forgiven.

7

Complete Coverage

One day while I was waiting for a stoplight to change, the Lord gave me a live demonstration of the work of Jesus Christ in dying to free us from the Law.

Stay Tuned for the Adventures of Under-dog!

The busy intersection was one of those favorite places where motorcycle cops watch for people to run the red light. The "law" was sitting there, waiting, as I came down the street. He was poised behind a large truck ready to catch the first violator. Cars were zipping by in the other direction with the green light. While I was waiting for the light to change an amazing thing happened.

Across the street from me, and against the line of traffic, a large dog began to make his way between the moving cars. Drivers swerved, brakes screeched, horns honked, and tires squealed, but the dog finally made it safely to the corner. I looked up in my rear view mirror to see if the policeman had attempted to do anything. He hadn't even moved. With all that commotion he had no doubt witnessed the whole scene, but sat there motionless.

As I drove off, I began to wonder why the policeman didn't chase the dog. The dog had violated the law. He had run the red light, hadn't he?

Some scriptures that I had been studying began to come to my mind. "But now we have been released from the Law" (Rom. 7:6). "For Christ is the end of the law for righteousness to everyone who believes" (Rom. 10:4). "The Law of the Spirit of life in Christ Jesus has set you free from the Law of sin and death" (Rom. 8:2). As the Spirit began to speak to me through these verses, I began to understand my relationship to the Law and what Jesus had done on my behalf.

Just as the dog was not under the Law to obey traffic lights, since the cross I, too, am not under God's Law to keep it. That does not mean God's Law is not true, any more than the red light wasn't "true." It means that in Christ we are governed by something other than the Law.

The dog was free from the law because he was incapable of compliance. I am free from the Law because somebody has already complied with it *for me.* The dog was not lawless; he just did not have that particular law speaking to him. The dog's owner was responsible for his actions. Being free from the Law of God does not produce lawlessness. Rather, Jesus has my "papers" and has assumed responsibility for me.

The dog was free from the law because of ignorance. I cannot claim ignorance because God says He has written the Law upon our hearts and minds. I know what is of God and what is not. And the life of Jesus Christ within me produces righteousness apart from the Law, yet consistent with the Law. In other words, with Christ ruling my life I will find Him sending me through on green lights!

I am free because of what Jesus did on my behalf on the cross. He has set me free from the Law's impossible demands which constantly stand against me. Jesus' life and death so fulfilled all God's Law that through believing and trusting Him I can freely experience righteous life. As a believer I am *not* a better law-keeper. Rather I have become one who allows the Holy Spirit to keep on fulfilling within me all of God's requirements.

We read the Bible, and we see that God's standards are perfect. In our hearts we want to be godly people. Because much of our daily living in the outside world is based on achievement, we naturally find ourselves through human achievement trying to live up to God's standards. When we don't meet them we become frustrated and discouraged. We can't live with ourselves as failures, so when we fail we try again to meet God's laws and again fall short. It's a vicious circle of sin and self-condemnation.

Jean Paul Sartre said, "There is no exit from the human dilemma." Jesus said, "*I* am the way. *I* am the door."

Unbending the Bent

One day a friend and I were talking about what really makes people sin. He confessed to me that he was having problems with sex desires and lust. By his own admission he had become obsessed with the problem.

We began by analyzing what sin is. We saw that sin is rebellion against God. Adam and Eve rebelled against God and *sin* (in the singular) came into God's perfect world. We also discovered that *sins* (plural) are what result from the sin nature we inherited from Adam. Our daily sins illustrate the outworking of this nature of rebellion against God in all areas of our lives.

My friend said, "Well that's nothing new. I know I have all kinds of sins and rebellion. The question is why do I do them?" Again we looked into the Bible. We found that the reason he sinned was because he allowed the Law to be constantly speaking to him. We read Romans 7:5: "For while we were in the flesh, the sinful passions aroused by the Law were at work in the members of our body to produce fruit for death."

Then I asked him, "In view of that verse, what two things are necessary for you to sin?" He looked at the verse again and exclaimed, "I see it. My sinful passions and the Law."

You know there is just something down inside of

me that wants to sin. I see it in my experience and see it in God's Word." Luther called it "a bent to sin."

I showed him still another verse, "The sting of death is sin and the power of sin is the law" (1 Cor. 15:56). The power of sin is the Law speaking to our sinful passions. Jesus said, "But I say to you, that everyone who looks at a woman to lust for her he has committed adultery with her already in his heart" (Matt. 5:28). We look, the Law speaks, our sinful desires are aroused, and we sin. Paul said, "Because by the works of the Law no flesh shall be justified in His sight" (Rom. 3:20). If you *try* to keep the Law, your response will be sin.

Then my friend with a sigh of desperation said, "But where is the solution?"

Again we looked to the Bible, Romans 7:8: "Apart from the Law sin is dead." This means that if by faith we see ourselves as dead to the Law, that Law will not speak to us. Jesus has replaced Law, and grace abounds all the more.

Paul said, "For you are dead, and your life is hid with Christ in God" (Col. 3:3). We are dead men on furlough. What does a dead man do? Nothing. He neither sins, nor does he produce righteousness. He's just dead.

Part of our being dead is that we are dead to the Law. The Law cannot talk to dead people. Thus, though the Law goes on as being true, it has no jurisdiction over a dead man. We were declared "dead on arrival" when we came to Christ because of His work on the cross.

But Jesus did something about me being dead. In making me a new person, He brought me back from the dead to belong to Him. My *old* self, which was under the Law, is dead. My *new* self, which is indwelt by the Holy Spirit, has been declared alive. So the new you is under no obligation to keep the Law. The new you belongs uniquely to the Holy Spirit, and it is He who is your life. Thus, we walk in the reality of the Spirit, and not in the routine of the Law.

It's the Principle of the Thing

What do we mean by Law? Law, in addition to being a moral code, is also a *principle*. It is a repeatable principle like gravity. If you hold an object up high and let go of it, it will drop to the ground. Do it many times, and the same thing will happen. God's law, as a principle, works in like manner. If you allow the Law to speak to your sinful passions, you will repeatedly sin.

Paul said, "I would not have come to know sin except through the Law" (Rom. 7:7). A baby never knows what a sweet tastes like until someone gives him one. Then it is taken away, so he cries. "For through the Law comes the knowledge of sin." When we know the standards of God and don't keep them, we sin.

Now, here's a mind boggler. One reason the Law

was given was to make us sin more! "And the Law came in that the transgression might increase, but where sin increased, grace abounded all the more" (Rom. 5:20). Paul said, "But sin, taking opportunity through the commandment, produced in me coveting of every kind" (Rom. 7:8). He also said, "It was through the commandment [Law] sin became utterly sinful. The Law as a repeatable principle caused Paul to sin more as his sinful passions were aroused.

It's like the man who lives on the corner of your block. He puts up a sign in his front yard which reads KEEP OFF THE GRASS. What does that prompt you to do as you walk by his place and round the corner? The law works the same way. Though it is eternally true, because of man's nature to sin, law engenders disobedience and unrighteousness.

My friend and I were now beginning to see that Jesus set us free to just trust Him. It is not our job to keep the Law. Jesus Christ has already done that on our behalf. "For Christ is the end of the law for righteousness to everyone who believes" (Rom. 10:4). I am free from the Law speaking to my sinful passions to transfer my trust to Jesus while He does whatever the Law requires.

Something Has to Go

If God is going to remove sin from our experience, He will have to remove one of the two causes of sin: sinful passions or the Law. Which one has he removed?

We looked further in the Bible. "But now we have been released from the Law, having died to that by which we were bound, so that we serve in newness of the Spirit and not in oldness of the letter [Law]" (Rom. 7:6). God in His grace has released us from the Law. He has brought us out from under it. We are dead to the Law and alive unto Christ.

Sure we have sinful passions, but they are aroused when we allow the Law to speak to them. Now we know that when the Law does speak to us, we have all the more reason to trust Christ to fulfill it.

My friend began to see the picture of the dog at the stoplight. He saw that just like the dog, we are free from the Law. It is the responsibility of our owner, Jesus Christ, to fulfill the Laws of God for us.

So this means we are not free from the Law to try and make it on our own. Removing us from the Law was only half the job. It is great to be free! It is great to have the Law fulfilled. But God does not leave us to our own devices. He has provided us with the Holy Spirit to bring out that fulfilled law (righteousness) within us.

The late Watchman Nee, the Chinese Christian leader, says it well in his book, *Table in the Wilderness.* "Now that I am in Christ, God's moral demands have not altered, but it is no longer I who meets them. Praise God, He who is the lawgiver on the Throne is now also the Lawkeeper in my heart. He who gave the Law himself keeps it. He makes the demands, but He also meets them. While we were trying to do it all, He could do nothing. It was because we were struggling to achieve it that we failed and failed. The trouble with us was that we were weak enough not to do the will of God, but not yet weak enough to keep out of things altogether. Only utter disillusion can throw men back in despair upon the God who is ready to do it all."

In Philippians 2:13 Paul says, "It is God who is at work in you, both to will and to work for His good pleasure."

When we believe in Christ as Savior, the Law has fulfilled its purpose. The Law has driven us to Christ. Galatians 3:24 says that the Law in our schoolmaster to lead us to Christ. We now have a diploma of righteousness and do not need the schoolmaster any longer. Paul states, "But now that faith has come, we are no longer under a schoolmaster." This freedom, then, does not lead to lawlessness. This freedom gets us out of the Law and into the Holy Spirit.

The "Angry Old Man"

I remember getting ready to teach a seminar at a conference grounds. A very angry man came towards me and asked if he could be in my classroom. I had seen him around the grounds and was aware of his bad attitude toward everyone. It was selfish on my part, but I did not want him disturbing my class. So I suggested that because my session was crowded he join another group down the hall. He left in a huff, but a few moments later returned and stood in the door with arms crossed and said, "I like your topic better."

He joined the class and sat in the front row glaring at me. After the session was over he came up and said, "I want to talk to you." It was mid-afternoon and I had other responsibilities during the next few hours, so I suggested we meet in my classroom at five o'clock. I left the building, and I sensed the Law speaking to me: "Love your neighbor as yourself."

The Law was getting to my sinful passions condemning me for not loving and accepting this angry man. My attitude at that point was anything but love towards him. But as I walked along, I said to God, "I cannot even like that guy. I'm going to trust your Spirit to love him through all that I am."

The Law says, "You do it." The Spirit says, "I will do it."

When we met again at five o'clock, *I* was different. I really loved that angry dude. I sensed an attitude change toward him. God had taken my intellect, emotion, and will—my personality—and loved through me.

As we talked, I found myself answering his questions and problems. God not only gave me love, but wisdom in the Spirit to answer his questions.

That's what it means to me to be free. We are not under the "yoke of slavery" to do it. We trust the Spirit to bring the love of Christ from within us. I found that I did not have to produce love; I was just free to navigate in the Holy Spirit. Freedom in Christ *produces* holiness.

Mirror, Mirror on the Wall

Now as I look into the Bible, I see it as a mirror to me. I read something that tells me to do something. Rather than try in the flesh to do it, I trust the Holy Spirit to make that true in my experience. When I see something that God says I should be doing, I now see it as a portrait of what I can expect God to do through me. The Word now becomes a mirror image of future happenings.

We have been programmed to think, "If the Law is obeyed, then God responds in grace." For so long I used to think, "If I do what God wants me to do, then He will be good to me." I became obsessed with keeping the Law so that God would bless.

Finally I began to understand that the grace of God was sufficient for *all* my needs. He admonished me to pray without ceasing. But I did not know that that came purely as a result of my relationship—not the cause. I began to see the Law not as something I must do to *receive* grace; the Law exposes my *need* of grace. The grace-controlled life becomes a life of living and responding to the Savior who is ready to do it all.

Paul asks the question in Romans 3: "Do we then nullify the Law through faith?" His own answer was, "May it never be! On the contrary, we establish the

Law." Living by the Grace of God does not produce lawlessness. It shows me my need of utter dependence upon God to produce His life through me. I can now pass through life unafraid of a "traffic-cop God" who will arrest me when I fail to keep the Law. Rather, I see Christ as the one who keeps me from failing by His life within me.

By the way, several months after talking to my friend with the lust problem, we met again. He eagerly told me of how he had begun to experience a whole new attitude toward sex and lustful desire. The Holy Spirit had replaced it with the reality of Christ. He told how this was true not only in this area, but in other areas of his life as well. It was evident to me that he had become free from the Law to become a really free person.

Martin Luther said: "A Christian is not somebody who has not sinned, but somebody against whom God no longer chalks sin because his faith is in Christ. This doctrine gives comfort to the consciences in trouble. When a person is a Christian, he is above Law and sin. When the Law accuses him and sin wants to drive the wits out of him, a Christian looks at Christ. A Christian is free. He has no master but Christ. A Christian is greater than the whole world."

Our coverage is complete!

8

Where Faith Begins

A long time ago I realized that God expects me to do the natural things of life, and He will take care of the supernatural. Now, let me explain that statement *fast,* or it might not sound correct!

Living the Christian life *anytime* is a supernatural event. If Jesus could not do anything apart from the Father, how much more do we need to trust Him! As I walk in dependence upon the Lord, I do my daily work through the natural talents, abilities, and experience He has already given me. I walk with Him and do what comes naturally. I can then expect that as God controls my life He will do the supernatural.

Called on the Carpet

We were finishing up the interiors of an important new bank branch, and the opening was set for about one week away. I was ready to install the carpeting but was notified that it hadn't been shipped from the factory. It really jolted me. My first thought was, What! a bank opening without carpet?

That evening as I drove home I talked the whole matter over with the Lord. I remember saying to Him, "Well, Lord, I've kept a good tab on the furniture and draperies, and they are here for delivery. I expected the carpet to be here, but it isn't. You know my heart, Lord, I have done everything that I could humanly do. Announcements for the open house are out. That can't be changed. So I'm asking You to do something that will bring honor to Your Name. Thank you for this problem—I'm just going to trust you."

The next day was busy and I was away from the office. When I returned the following day, there was a phone message from the carpet installer. I called him.

"We have this roll of carpet we can't seem to identify," he said. "Can you stop by and see if it is yours?"

On the way home I stopped by his place and checked. Sure enough. It was the carpet ordered for the bank. Somehow the information from the factory was incorrect, and the carpet was already in Seattle.

The bank opening came off with a beautifully completed interior—carpet and all.

Many times I have given the Lord the credit for doing the supernatural in that bank problem. This same thing has happened concerning personal finances, employee relationships, sales opportunities, and slumps.

Paul says that God can "do exceeding abundantly above all that we ask or think."

Objection Overruled

I remember an experience while I lived in San Francisco. We were competing for a $30,000 order for a new office addition to a factory. The purchasing agent was one known to take money on the side to favor one seller over another. You know, deals like that are so tempting, but what a thrill to walk in Christ and let Him do it.

We made our presentation to the buying committee and submitted our price proposal. I followed up on our offer regularly.

The day before the company was to make their final decision I met with the purchasing agent to review our bid. He was cool, and I left feeling that somebody's money was talking to him.

As I drove across the Bay Bridge, I reflected on the little meeting we had had. I began to pray and to praise God for the experience I had in dealing honestly with the buyer. I remember in my prayer I just told God how grateful I was to just walk by faith—weak though it was—and said to Him, "Lord, if I'm going to get the order, you're going to have to be the salesman."

The next day I was ill and didn't even make it to work. The office called to say that the buyer had phoned several times. I returned the calls.

He said in a rather offensive way, "I don't know how you did it, but you got the order. The committee over-ruled my choice in your favor. Come on by when you're back on your feet, and we will settle the order."

I am not trying to say that God works only when we are in trouble. I am saying that God is vitally interested in *everything* that confronts us.

On the Rocks, or on the Rock?

Often, while on business trips, I am faced with a situation or event that is foreign to my lifestyle at home. But even in strange surroundings, God can be trusted to work the unexpected.

While at a convention in Chicago I attended a cocktail party for a particular supplier. It was a chance to get acquainted with some of the traveling salesmen. Several of us were talking together in a group.

As I was finishing my Coke and about to leave, one of the men followed me to the door. He said, "Ken, you said something a minute ago I would like to talk to you about." I suggested we talk right then and we headed for the coffee shop.

Over coffee he reminded me of something I had said about my relationship to God that, frankly, I had not even remembered saying. A simple statement had made such an impression on him that he wanted to know more about how he could become a Christian. We talked openly about Jesus Christ, and I shared the gospel with him. Several weeks later at home he invited Christ to be his Savior.

This was an example to me of how God does the supernatural in a natural situation. As we live by His life, He is free to use our lips, our hands for whatever He desires—sometimes without our even realizing it.

He has promised to give us the desires of our hearts. We can really trust Him to do this. We ask God for our desires and if He takes the desire away we know it wasn't meant to be. In this way we can just live by faith, trusting Him to do for us whatever we really need.

Seeing Isn't Always Believing

The Scripture says that "We walk by faith and not by sight" (2 Cor. 5:7). It's a matter of attitude. So much of Christian life, I feel, is a matter of whom do I choose to trust? If I try to do it, I fail. If the Holy Spirit is permitted free access, wholeness and joy is a by-product.

And sometimes the answer is, "No."

Several years ago I was faced with an option that would alter the whole course of my life. God had worked before concerning some other decisions of magnitude, and I believed I could trust Him here. I was to decide whether or not to leave my business and go into Christian work on a full-time basis.

I had been praying about the decision for some time and was waiting on God to give me His peace. I have found that when I have peace about a matter I can move out and know I am moving according to

God's will. Many times there have been several "good things" from which to choose. If confusion comes, I do nothing at all. Satan is the author of confusion. God is the author of peace.

One day as I was reading the Scriptures, God spoke to me concerning my leaving the business. He made it so clear that I began to make plans to leave Seattle and move my family to this new opportunity. We put our home up for sale, left our business interests, and moved our furniture and family into a modest house 1500 miles away. Through this whole adventure God performed so many exciting supernatural events that He again conclusively proved to us He is worthy of our trust.

But the aspect that was of interest here was that we could not sell our home in Seattle. Sometimes it was a very big question mark to us. We had asked the Lord to sell the house many times—why were we unable to do so? His answer was just plain, "No."

We rented it out and continued to trust Him for the sale some day, but it never sold. As always, He had a reason.

Five years later, when we left the organization to begin working in the Evangelism Department of the American Lutheran Church, we moved back into our "Old Seattle Home." *God had been saving it for us.* We had literally been forced to trust Him for this unanswered prayer, and He in His wisdom worked it out better than we could ever have planned it ourselves.

Throughout the years I have learned that faith begins to become a reality in life as we just allow God to be God and don't try to help Him out. Faith adds nothing to what God has done or will do. It just gives God the opportunity to make what He has already done true and alive in our experience.

9

Thou Shalt Not Sweat It

If I were to sum up the Christian life in two words it would be TRUST GOD. Yet for many it is hard to trust God. It may be hard for you also. True, but there is a reason. To help you see why, answer these questions.

Question one: Whom do you trust the most in a human sense? Yourself? Your partner in marriage? Your parents? Usually one of these is the case.

Question two: Why do you trust that person the most? Obviously it is because you know him the best.

Question three: Then why don't people trust God? Because they do not know Him. They don't know He loves them as He does, so they have a hangup about trusting Him for fear their lack of love won't merit His love. They don't know they are forgiven, so every-time sin appears in their lives they are afraid God is going to get even with them, or their penance won't be enough to earn their forgiveness.

Trust or Bust!

People are unable to trust a God who they think expects them to produce the Christian life. Everytime they fail, they sense an alienation from God. It is naturally hard to trust someone you don't know.

But conversely, when I began to trust God for His love, forgiveness, and power in all things, I began to experience my faith grow. I began to see I could trust God in areas I never did before.

I have found in my business life I could trust God to be very much a part of every day. The Christian life for me became a way of living. He influenced my decisions, He became my honesty, He controlled my temperament, He gave me wisdom whenever I needed it. He was my business life. As Paul said, "For me living is Christ." I found that the more I trusted God the more He rewarded me in all areas.

God wants us to trust Him not only for spiritual things but for everything. *Everything.* He says, "As you have therefore received Christ Jesus the Lord, so walk in Him" (Col. 2:6). We receive Christ as our Savior by faith, and He wants us to live that way too. "And whatever you do in word or deed, do all in the name of the Lord Jesus" (Col. 3:17). I am convinced by experience that the faith it takes to live the Christian life is to believe God will not tell you a lie, that He will do what He says in the Bible, the catalog of God's promises to men.

But even our trusting can become a work of the

flesh. We can even reason, "All this sounds so good, I've got to believe it." So we begin to work at believing. In fact, we begin to pressure ourselves to try and believe beyond our faith. God says He gives to each a measure of faith (Rom. 12:3). He says the faith you have, have as your own conviction before God (Rom. 14:22). Everyone reading this book has spiritual faith at some level. Ephesians 2:8-9 say faith is a gift from God. We don't pump up faith for each time we need it. We live in faith and allow God to produce more faith as we need it.

For years I lived having faith in my faith. I would take my spiritual temperature based upon how much faith I had. Some days I felt I did not have enough faith to live the Christian life. My problem was I had my eyes on the means instead of the object—the source.

It is like looking at the view from the front window of our home. We can see the Puget Sound below us and the Olympic Mountain range beyond the Sound. Boats and ferries pass by regularly. Now if I were to begin to describe the beauty of that scene by saying, "I have good vision, I have two eyes in my head, I see with them, they are brown and I don't need glasses to see the view," would I have described the scene? No, I would have been talking about the means by which I see the view—my eyes. I did not describe the object, I described the means by which I see the object to describe it. Likewise we sometimes attend to the means —faith—rather than to the object of our faith—the

84

Triune God. And God wants us to trust Him where we can trust, not where we cannot.

The 11th Commandment

One day as I was explaining this simple walk of faith to a group of teenagers, one of them piped up, "Well, that sounds good for you. You've been a Christian a long time. But what happens if I sincerely trust God and nothing happens?"

She presented me with a problem I had never given much thought to. It seemed to me that part of faith was to go on trusting God whether He worked or not. As I breathed a prayer to God for an answer to this sincere question, I asked her to look at a verse in Philippians with me.

"Be anxious for nothing," the verse started out, "but in everything by prayer and supplication with thanksgiving let your requests be made known to God. And the peace of God which passes all comprehension shall guard your hearts and your minds in Christ Jesus" (Phil. 4:6-7).

I asked the young Christian what this meant to her. After a few moments of looking at the verse in deep thought, a smile enlightened her face and she exclaimed, "That means don't sweat it—Jesus will work it out."

The whole group understood immediately. I had learned an old truth from a contemporary statement by a relatively new Christian. The phrase, *Don't Sweat*

It became almost a slogan among us. In fact, one girl I was counselling later heard me say it so many times that when she came to really believe it, she made me a banner containing a cross and the letters D.S.I. It is hanging in our hall at home today.

Later at a church-related college we were discussing faith and the Law. It was there that the expression "The Eleventh Commandment" was coined for me by a student. He said it very simply. "What you are saying to us, Ken, is that God does it all, and we can just live by the Eleventh Commandment, 'Thou shalt not sweat it.' "

Food for the Fed-Up

During her sixteenth year, one of my daughters and I were talking just before she went to bed one evening. She told me she was fed up with Christianity and wanted nothing more to do with it. She had intellectually come to the place where she had chosen to reject all the Christian training and teaching she had received in our home and church.

We talked about her right to reject God if she wanted to. I told her that no matter what she ever did —even to blaspheming God—it would not change my love for her. I asked her to keep everything in balance and not throw out what she had learned about God and Jesus Christ while she began to investigate new philosophies.

As I went into our bedroom, I explained to Doris what our daughter had decided. I related her decision and my reaction. Doris expressed my sentiments thoroughly when she said simply, "I guess we will just have to trust God, won't we?" As we prayed that evening we completely entrusted our girl into God's hands to bring her to Himself. At that point our faith very honestly was not strong enough to cope with the situation. We claimed God's promises and trusted Him to work (the Eleventh Commandment).

Two weeks later the family attended a Bible camp in Canada. I was one of the speakers for the high school camp. Our girls came along—one reluctantly. During that week at camp the rebellious daughter after seeing the reality of Christ in the life of some of the young Christians made a secret commitment to Him. None of us was aware of her decision.

Following a noon-time camp out on a mountain side, some of the kids decided to climb to the top of the mountain. Our daughter was among them. Late that afternoon as I looked at the mountain from the Bible Camp below I saw a forest fire on the mountain side. "Our kids are above the fire" was my first thought.

I borrowed a car and drove up the mountain as far as I could. Firefighters and apparatus were already on the scene. As I followed the road through the woods, I came upon my daughter and two other girls resting in a car. They expressed their relief at being safe and their concern for the three fellow-climbers now fighting the fire.

We returned to the camp and spread the good news

that all the hikers were safe. That evening as we gathered for devotions the girls related how the Lord had brought them out through the fire safely.

Later our daughter shared with us how in seeing the faith of the other kids in that situation caused her to see the reality of trusting God. Though she was frightened and even feared death, the combined faith of these young believers gave her the strength to meet the problem.

God gave us the faith to trust His Holy Spirit to work in her life rather than to try to do it ourselves. So often we want to make things happen, that in our desire to see our kids enjoy the life of Christ we drive them further away. Our faith increased as a result of this experience of learning to trust God and not sweat it.

Father Knew Best

Throughout my life I have always seen my Dad as a real example of faith. He never seemed to have much material wealth, but was rich toward God. Many times I saw how it was Dad's trust of God that brought us through many a crisis.

During the last three years of his life, Dad's health failed through emphysema and bronchial complications. Mom dedicated her time to care for him during those long days and longer nights. Many times Dad would suffer at night from pain, lack of sleep, and improper breathing. His body deteriorated, but his mind and heart and spirit were triumphant.

My folks carried on a ministry of prayer for both my brother and me. When I would go out to share Christ with others, Dad insisted on knowing at what hour I would be speaking so that he could pray for me. If I was in another time zone, he would adjust his watch for his intercessory time.

Many times I would call on the phone to see how things were going with my parents. When Dad would come on the phone I would inquire about his health and his answer always was, "Never mind that, tell me what God is doing in the meeting." He knew the Lord would answer his prayers. It never occurred to Dad to question the Lord.

During my father's last year of confinement, the television often provided his Sunday worship. He would watch many of the programs that were provided for the shut-in person. Several of these were programs that included times of prayer for healing of the sick. Dad would join them in prayer and would weep with joy as people told of their bodies being healed by the Lord. But even though Dad had faith in all of God's promises, God never chose to heal him of his illness.

Several days before my father died, I was at my parents' home. That afternoon I was sitting in the backyard soaking up some sun. Because the load was heavy on my mother, we had nurses around the clock to care for Dad. He always knew what was going on, and that morning as I had arrived from Denver, low as he was, he insisted I tell him all about the meetings that week.

As I was dozing in the sunlight, Mom called and said, "the nurse said Dad wants to see us. Come on in quick." I bolted into the house and upstairs to his bedroom, expecting to witness his death. He was propped up in his bed and I saw on his face a peaceful, almost angelic expression that I had never seen before.

I went over by the bed and sat down on a chair and took his hand. He could only say, "It was beautiful. It was wonderful."

"What was, Dad?" I asked.

"God was here in the room and everything was so beautiful." All he could do was tell us that he had seen and experienced something that he could not even begin to describe. Something that he didn't want to leave. He kept saying, "God was here. It was so beautiful, so wonderful."

The nurse began to explain what had happened. She had been trained in Roman Catholic hospitals to watch for these spiritual experiences when patients near death. She explained that as she was watching Dad, his face seemed to change from the twitching and grimaces that accompany death to a glowing peaceful smile. She went to his side and took his hand and began to pray the Lord's Prayer with him. Dad had told her previously of his faith in Christ, and she knew he was having a special experience with the

Lord. She had called Mom and me to experience the joy of that moment.

I am convinced that God gave him a preview of what heaven is like. He gave him an assurance that his pain and suffering would not be long. He had been caught up in the Spirit.

As we sat there, my father seemed to try to look off into the distance to regain the experience. We all felt he must be dying. "It was beautiful, it was wonderful," he repeated. "But you can all go now, I'm not going to die yet."

On the day he died, my mother tells of talking to him early in the morning. Dad said to her, "It's hard to die." Mom asked him what he meant. He said, "It's hard to die because you can't go as soon as you want to. God doesn't take you until He is ready." In life and death Dad was "anxious for nothing."

Dad's funeral, by the way, was a time of celebration. Many came to express their love for this man. Dad was with the Lord and his healing was complete. Through my dad, I was given a live, full-color demonstration of what God means when He says, "But the righteous man shall live by faith" (Rom. 1:17).

10

A New Reformation

Nearly five hundred years ago in Germany, an Augustinian monk named Martin Luther while examining the Scriptures came to a new awareness that justification was through faith in Jesus Christ alone. Luther found through his own experience that God's work within him did not qualify him to be accepted in the sight of God. In all sincerity he had followed the teachings and practice of his church but found no personal freedom in his relationship to God, nor enough righteousness or goodness in himself to face God. He saw no hope of salvation on personal merit.

Luther discovered that Christ's work of dying and meeting God's requirements on our behalf was the only basis by which God accepts us. He had seen what his man-centered, experience-centered, mind-centered, feelings-oriented, religious life had produced. Luther discovered that he was justified before God only by God's grace in Christ. It was not by what he did or even by God's grace in his heart, but solely by what Jesus did on the cross.

In discovering this truth, Luther unknowingly spurred a Reformation in the church that was Christ-centered, cross-centered, and caused believers to look outside their experience to Jesus alone for their salvation.

There's a New Day Coming

Today as I travel throughout North America, I am convinced we need a new reformation. Certainly the message of salvation by faith in Christ is being shared and people are being converted. The reformation and change in the lives of people is tremendous.

But what I am talking about is a different kind of reformation—a reformation that says and teaches that the Christian life is lived by faith in Jesus Christ alone, a reformation that says that I look beyond my experience arising from my senses, and by faith accept the finished work of Christ on my behalf. Luther saw through the error of *salvation by works;* today let us similarly discard the subtle *sanctification by works* still present in so many lives.

So often I meet people who have come out from the "bonds of sin" to become Christians only to go right back into the "bonds of legalism." In many cases this has a worse effect on them than the first. We seem to feel that because we are Christians we must *do* something to maintain being a Christian. Satan lies to us and causes us to look at our experiences, and we see ourselves guilty of not meeting God's standards.

You Can't Earn a Gift

In Ohio recently I had a beautiful experience following a meeting. A woman with whom I was talking received Christ as her Savior. She had shared the frustrations of her life concerning her church experience and inability to get her husband "involved."

After we prayed together I asked her, "What are you going to do about your new life in Christ?"

"I don't know," she answered, "but I will try to work towards being a good Christian."

Isn't it interesting that she was so programmed religiously that even after giving her life to Christ by sheer faith, she was now going to reassume the control of her life? It was a joy to show her that the biggest mistake we make as believers is when we depend on "I." Everytime we trust "I," we assume that either we have to do it all, or at least *help* God to work it out.

We discussed that as far as God was concerned, her work of salvation was all completed. She did not have to try to make the Christian life happen. God had done his work of grace for her through Christ. All He wanted from her was for her to trust Him.

I compared what had just happened to her with the birth of a new baby. The human infant is one of the most helpless creatures ever born. He can do nothing for himself, except cry out for help. Without realizing what he is doing he completely trusts in his parents to feed him, clothe him, love him, wash him, and change his dirty diapers.

In the same way that is all God wants from us. He knows we are helpless to live the Christian life. He too wants us to trust in Him completely. He will feed us when we are hungry. He will clothe us with His righteousness, He will continually love us no matter how messy our diapers. He does all this because we are justified by God's own work of grace in Jesus.

The next evening the lady returned to the meeting and presented me with a poem she had written. She had become so freed in her spirit that she could not sleep and had written what was on her heart. In her trust of God—her faith—He had released her from the burdens of life and her poem was filled with a sense of release.

This woman experienced the freedom that a life of faith always produces. Yet so many of us are still programmed to feel we must be "doing" rather than just "believing." We have been so used to earning everything in life that it is easy for us to begin working for a deeper spiritual life.

Wholly Holy

We cannot make ourselves sanctified. We are sanctified by God alone through Jesus Christ. Sanctification —being made holy—comes only by faith. It is not what I do that sanctifies me. It is what Jesus has done for me through His blood.

Paul says this to the Christians at Corinth: "To the church of God which is at Corinth, to those who have been sanctified in Christ Jesus, saints by calling" (1 Cor. 1:2). Why could he call them saints? Because they were made holy through Jesus.

Later, Paul makes it even clearer. After telling them about what kind of people they were, he says, "And such were some of you, but you were washed, but you were sanctified, but you were justified in the name of the Lord Jesus Christ and in the Spirit of our God. The previous—and in some cases, even current—bad habits of these weak Corinthian Christians were still no match for the finished work of Jesus! Paul told them forcefully that they were now washed by Jesus' blood, sanctified by Jesus, and justified by Jesus Christ.

So often in my life I have to reflect on this important truth. Sometimes I forget the fact that these things are true about me. In doing so I deny the truth of God, and the result is I fail to experience my freedom in Christ.

As with Luther, we need to stand confidently on the fact that we are what we are *only* on the basis of what Jesus Christ has done.

Paul says to us in Col. 2:6, "As you have therefore received Christ Jesus the Lord, so walk in Him." We received Jesus as our Saviour by faith. We are instructed to walk (or live) in Him the same exact way —by faith.

The Avis Rent-a-Car Christian

"We try harder" is a famous slogan of the admittedly number-two car rental firm. Let's scrap the concept of being "number two" type Christians who live by trying harder.

God says that we are to live by faith. "For without faith it is impossible to please God, for he who comes to God must believe that He is and is a rewarder of those who seek Him" (Heb. 11:6). God is pleased with faith.

How often we have to be reminded that it is God who promises. Our response therefore before such an awesome truth is simply to trust Him. Now when we trust Him to keep those promises, we honor Him by that faith and He in turn counts me as righteous.

My Christian life is therefore characterized by one word, TRUST. Accordingly I do not please God by "the Christian things" I do. I do not please God if I read the Bible. What pleases Him is when I trust the promises I read in the Word. He is not pleased by my prayers unless they express my trust and praise to Him. He is pleased when my prayers claim His promises by faith. It means nothing to God that I exercise my spiritual gift. Letting the Holy Spirit work through me as I trust Him completely really does.

Do you see the difference? When we see that it is not *our acts* that please the Lord, but rather our total dependence upon Him, then we experience the blessing that comes from reading the Bible, praying, or seeing the work of the Spirit in our lives.

The Faith & Trust Company

There is a fine line between faith and trust as I see it. Mark tells the story of Jesus and His disciples as they were together crossing the Sea of Galilee. Jesus was tired and took a nap on a cushion in the stern of the boat.

"And there arose a fierce gale of wind and the waves were breaking over the boat so much that the boat was already filling up." They then woke Jesus up and said to Him, "Teacher, do you not care that we are perishing?" Jesus stood and rebuked the wind and waves and "It became perfectly calm."

Then Jesus said to them, "Why are you so timid? How is it that you have no faith?" What Jesus is saying here is simply, "It was my will for you to be here in this boat. Why can't you trust me?"

The disciples had *faith* in Jesus their Lord but they could not *trust* Him to wake up. So they cried out in fear.

Often we believers have faith in God for our salvation but cannot trust God for the everyday life. As one man said to me, "I can sure trust Him for the big things. It's the small ones I have problems trusting Him for." That is so true of so many of us. We are programmed to make things happen by ourselves. But in Christ we are new people. Old habit patterns begin to drop off. Whereas before we did everything on our own, we now begin to see the truth in Jesus' words, "For apart from me you can do nothing" (John 15:5).

There is no satisfaction or fulfillment in trusting past experiences. I can recall an evening with some other believers. We experienced a powerful anointing of the Holy Spirit on our gathering. Our relationship of love was exhilarating. It truly was as though we were at Pentecost. Yet, later in the week some of us were at odds with each other over theological differences. Where was our love and spiritual anointing?

It was then that I realized that the only *lasting* experience I can have is the reality of Jesus Christ through day by day trust. My joy and peace with God comes only by faith, not by what I have experienced in the past.

Even my heart and my mind are untrustworthy. They are deceitful and desperately wicked. Satan can confront my mind with his lies. But life for the Christian is believing that God has not told a lie; that our salvation is in Jesus Christ *alone;* that our justification is through Jesus Christ *alone;* that our sanctification is in Jesus Christ *alone.* All the work of Christ has been done *outside* of my life and it's completed. Therefore I do not need to look anymore at my experience but to Jesus Christ.

We need a new reformation of Grace. We need to recycle the message of the sixteenth century reformation—and amplify it to say that the righteousness in Christian living is only by faith in what the Father has done for us through Christ. Only by Christ. The Son alone knows how to live the Christian life, and He is currently doing it in all who trust Him through His Holy Spirit.

"Being justified as a gift by His Grace through the redemption which is in Christ Jesus; whom God displayed publicly as a propitiation in His blood through faith. This was to demonstrate His righteousness, because in the forbearance of God He passed over the sins previously committed" (Rom. 3:24-25).

This is the reformation we need. And you know what? It's happening!

STUDY GUIDE

Use of This Study Guide

This material has been prepared for use both in small groups and for individual readers. Its purpose is to amplify what has been said in these pages through direct biblical references and questions to encourage further thought and discussion. For greatest clarity of study, read over the appropriate chapter of this book and Bible passages carefully just before answering the questions.

1. Our Spiritual Portfolio

Biblical references: Ephesians 1:3-23; 1 Corinthians 1:4-10

1. Why do you think that Christians often tend to live by *feelings* instead of by *faith?* What has God done for you to help you and others reverse this attitude?

2. Think through on what you have become in Christ. Name some of these truths and what they mean to you.

3. In what ways do you see yourself differently than you did before reading Chapter One?

2. What's in a Name?

Biblical references: John 3:1-8; Ephesians 2:8-9; Revelation 3:20

1. In your opinion, what is involved in becoming a Christian? How does your answer compare with the content of the above references—similarities and dissimilarities?

2. Have you experienced "sidetracks" similar to the author's experience? What were they? What solutions do you believe the Word of God has to give for these matters?

3. What does the phrase, "Jesus has to do it all" mean to you in your own Christian life? If you have never accepted Jesus Christ as your own Savior and Lord, will you do so today?

3. Where Love Begins

Biblical references: Luke 19:1-10; John 8:1-11; John 13:36-38

1. With whom do you relate best in this chapter: Zaccheus, the prostitute (no offense!), or Peter? Why?

2. How have other Christians you know helped you to believe and experience the unconditional love of God?

3. How would you express God's love to: a. a person high on drugs b. a bigot c. an adulterer—even if you saw no guaranteed hope of change in these people?

4. Getting a Head in the World

Biblical references: Ephesians 5:22-23, 1 Corinthians 12:12-27

1. Your head controls your body; Jesus, as Head, controls His body. The question: How? In what ways?

2. Have you experienced the guidance or "headship" of Jesus Christ in a group situation, that is, *where He is really leading the group?* Describe this experience, relating it to and comparing it with I Corinthians 12:12-27.

3. In a group situation, what do you feel are some ways that you can experience more of the actual headship of Christ?

5. Why Love Is Possible

Biblical references: Hebrews 10:1-22; 1 John 2:1-2

1. Explain how a consciousness of sin in your life has caused you to have a bogus life-style.

2. Why does Jesus, our High Priest, continue to remain in the heavenly Holy of Holies? What is His ministry there?

3. Has reading this chapter helped liberate your mind from a consciousness of sin? What has God taught you in this regard?

6. It's Just Not the Issue

Biblical references: Acts 10:43; Romans 8:1-2; 2 Corinthians 5:17-21

1. Why does Satan want us to be sin-centered in our daily living?

2. Why is it possible for God to look at me and see me as righteous as Jesus Christ?

3. Will walking by faith and forgetting sin as God has caused you to live a loose and sinful life? Explain.

7. Complete Coverage

Biblical references: Colossians 2:12-15; Romans 7:5—8:11; Galatians 2:20-21

1. In what way was God's Law fulfilled in you?

2. Are we to become anti-Law or lawless as believers? What does it mean to trust the Holy Spirit apart from the Law?

3. Explain how God's grace never changes towards believers, regardless of their weaknesses or failures.

8. Where Faith Begins

Biblical references: Hebrews 11; Romans 10:10; 2 Corinthians 5:7

1. Does God answer our prayers to the measure of the faith we generate?

2. When we see God give a "no" answer to our prayers, does this mean that we are to pray harder? Think back to some situations where God has said "no," and discuss what is an appropriate response.

3. What does it mean to you to walk by faith, not by sight?

9. Thou Shalt Not Sweat It

Biblical references: Philippians 4:6-8; Psalm 23; Philippians 2:12-13

1. Is trusting God moment by moment a cop-out from the problems of daily life and how we face them? Explain.

2. Should we force other people to attend church, read the Bible, do Christian things when they don't want to? If not, what is the alternative?

3. If God has a predetermined time schedule, how does our trusting Him fit in?

10. A New Reformation

Biblical references: Romans 3:24-25; Luke 23:39-47

1. What is the basis of salvation: God's work of grace inside of you or God's work of grace on the cross of Jesus Christ? Which is "cause," which is "effect"? Why is this distinction important?

2. Do you sense we need a new Reformation? What do you feel are some areas of change today that God wants to make in His people?

3. What gifts and ministries (modes of service) do you feel God has given you to help spread the good news of Jesus Christ?